LANGUAGE ARTS EXPLORER JUNIOR

How to Write a Lab Report

by Nel Yomtov

CHERRY LAKE PUBLISHING · ANN ARBOR, MICHIGAN

Published in the United States of America by Cherry Lake Publishing
Ann Arbor, Michigan
www.cherrylakepublishing.com

Content Adviser: Gail Dickinson, PhD, Associate Professor,
Old Dominion University, Norfolk, Virginia

Photo Credits: Page 4, ©Rob Marmion/Shutterstock, Inc.; page 5, ©Lisa
F. Young/Shutterstock, Inc.; page 6, ©Ijansempoi/Shutterstock, Inc.; page
7, ©Markus Mainka/Shutterstock, Inc.; page 14, ©Pavel L Photo and
Video/Shutterstock, Inc.; page 16, ©karelnoppe/Shutterstock, Inc.; page
20, ©Sergey Novikov/Shutterstock, Inc.

Library of Congress Cataloging-in-Publication Data
Yomtov, Nelson.
  How to write a lab report / by Nel Yomtov.
     pages cm. — (Language arts explorer junior)
  Includes bibliographical references and index.
  ISBN 978-1-62431-185-7 (library binding) —ISBN 978-1-62431-251-9
(e-book) 1— ISBN 978-1-62431-317-2 (paperback). Technical writing—
Juvenile literature. 2. Report writing—Juvenile literature. 3. Science—
Experiments—Juvenile literature I. Title.

  T11.Y66 2013
  808.06'6—dc23   2013007047

Cherry Lake Publishing would like to acknowledge the work
of The Partnership for 21st Century Skills. Please visit www.p21.org
for more information.

Printed in the United States of America
Corporate Graphics, Inc.
July 2013
CLFA1

Table of Contents

CHAPTER ONE

Be a Super Scientist!

Have you ever done a science experiment?

Do you want to learn about the world around you? Studying science is one of the best ways to do it. It gives you a chance to figure things out through exciting hands-on exploration. There's nothing like the thrill of conducting your own experiments. You can do them in a laboratory at school. You can even do experiments at home!

But how do scientists keep track of their experiments? They write a document called a **lab report**. A lab report describes the findings of your research. It explains what you've discovered. It also details the conclusions you've made based on your findings. There is a method all scientists follow to conduct scientific experiments. It is called the scientific method.

Writing lab reports is an important part of experimenting.

CHAPTER TWO

The Scientific Method

The scientific method is a way to ask and answer questions. Scientists research and make **observations**. They also do experiments. There are generally five steps in the scientific method:

1. **Make an observation.** What things make you curious to learn more? You  may have observed that plants grow toward sunlight. Do you want to know why?

Have you ever looked closely at a plant?

Use the information you know to think up a hypothesis.

2. **Ask a question.** This narrows the focus of your observation. Why does the stem of a plant grow upward?

3. **Make a hypothesis.** A hypothesis is your best guess for an answer to your question. It is based on what you already know. You know that plants need sunlight to survive. Your hypothesis could be that plants grow upward to reach toward sunlight.

Make a List

Write down at least three hypotheses you would like to test. Think about what you already know. What do you want to learn about? Be creative! Here are some examples:

- Eating a good breakfast makes you more alert in the morning.
- Tomato plants grow faster when they receive more sunlight.
- Sugar dissolves more quickly in a hot liquid than in a cold liquid.

To get a copy of this activity, visit www.cherrylakepublishing.com/activities.

4. **Run an experiment.** Design an experiment. It will test your hypothesis. You could set up plants in different positions around light sources. Then you could see if the plants grow toward the light.

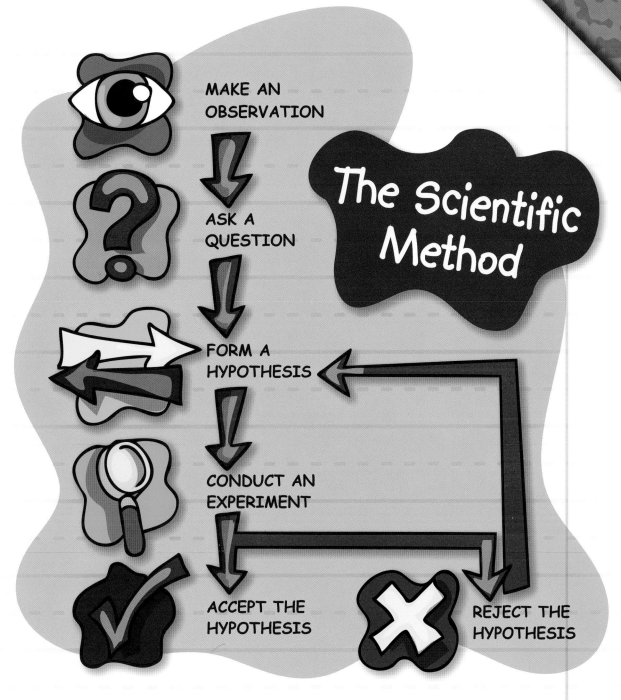

MAKE AN
OBSERVATION

ASK A
QUESTION

FORM A
HYPOTHESIS

The Scientific
Method

CONDUCT AN
EXPERIMENT

ACCEPT THE
HYPOTHESIS

REJECT THE
HYPOTHESIS

5. **Analyze your findings and draw a conclusion.** Study the results. Do they support your hypothesis?

CHAPTER THREE

Getting Started

You have completed your experiment.
Now it is time to write your lab report.
Take a look at this sample before you begin.

Sample Lab Report

Name: Kevin Somers

Date: February 4, 2014

Project Title: Testing How Mold Grows

Question (purpose or reason for my experiment):
I observed that mold grows on most types of food.
I wanted to know whether different temperatures or
weather conditions make mold grow. The question I want to
answer is: What conditions make mold grow best?

Hypothesis: Mold grows best in warm, moist, and dark
conditions.

Materials:
- 4 slices of white bread
- Water
- Plastic food wrap
- 2 paper bags
- 2 weeks of experiment time

Methods:
1. I sliced the first piece of bread in half. I wrapped
   one half in plastic food wrap. I left the other half
   unwrapped. Then I put them on my kitchen countertop.

2. I sliced the second piece of bread in half. I put one half in a paper bag and closed it up. I left the second half on a windowsill in sunlight.

3. I sliced the third piece of bread in half. I sprinkled water on one half every day. I left the other half dry.

4. I sliced the fourth piece of bread in half. I put half in a closed paper bag. I left the bag on the top of my refrigerator. It is warm there. I put the other half in the refrigerator. It is dark and cold there.

5. I examined all eight samples every day for two weeks. I recorded all the changes in the slices of bread.

Results (the findings of my experiment):

1. First piece of bread: The wrapped bread developed mold more slowly than the unwrapped bread.

2. Second piece of bread: The bread in the darkened paper bag grew mold more quickly than the bread left in the sunlight.

3. Third piece of bread: The wet bread developed mold more quickly than the dry bread.

4. Fourth piece of bread: The bread in the closed paper bag on top of the refrigerator developed mold more quickly than the bread in the refrigerator.

Conclusions:

1. Mold will eventually develop on all of the samples.
2. Mold grows best in warm, dark, and moist conditions.

Begin your report by explaining the purpose for your experiment. Write the question you want to **investigate** in this section. You can also explain why you want to conduct the experiment. This can be something you observed. It could also be something you read about.

State your hypothesis in the next section. Remember that a hypothesis is a guess. It predicts what you expect to happen. You should always include your original hypothesis in your lab report. Include it even if it is proven wrong by your experiment. An incorrect hypothesis can help provide you with new questions. You can use them in another experiment.

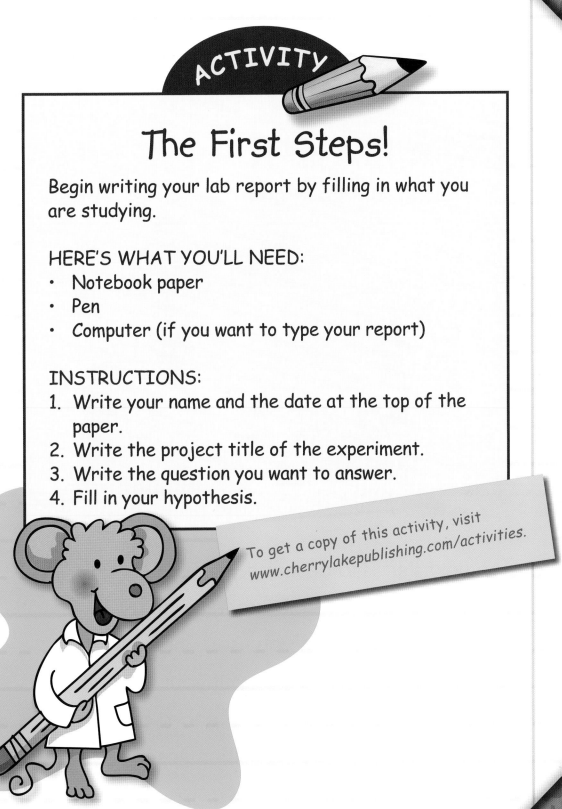

ACTIVITY

The First Steps!

Begin writing your lab report by filling in what you are studying.

HERE'S WHAT YOU'LL NEED:
- Notebook paper
- Pen
- Computer (if you want to type your report)

INSTRUCTIONS:
1. Write your name and the date at the top of the paper.
2. Write the project title of the experiment.
3. Write the question you want to answer.
4. Fill in your hypothesis.

To get a copy of this activity, visit www.cherrylakepublishing.com/activities.

CHAPTER FOUR

Describing Your Experiment

Keep careful track of the supplies you use.

The next step is to describe your experiment. This information explains the process you used. It includes the materials you used. It also includes the steps you took to carry out your experiment.

List all of your materials. Record how much of them you used. Be specific. Describe the amount in weight, length, or any other measurement you need. Include the brand name of the materials as well.

Now describe the steps you used to conduct the experiment. They should be listed in the exact order you did them. Your instructions should be clear enough to help others conduct your experiment just as you did. Include many details. Explain how long the experiment took. This section should also detail preparation work, such as labeling your materials.

ACTIVITY

Keep at It!

Continue to write your lab report. Add the list of materials you used. Also include the steps you used to conduct your experiment.

To get a copy of this activity, visit www.cherrylakepublishing.com/activities.

CHAPTER FIVE

Getting Results

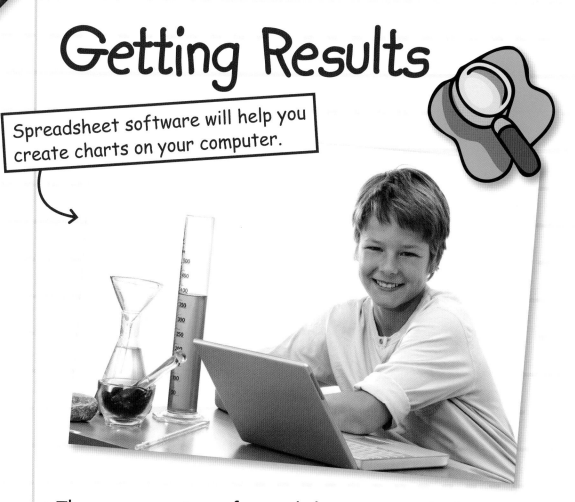

Spreadsheet software will help you create charts on your computer.

The next section of your lab report includes your results. This is where you include the **data** or measurements you recorded. You can include photographs or charts to help explain the data. This section presents your results directly. It does not discuss or explain your thoughts on the experiment's outcome.

Bar graphs are one of the most common types of graphs used in lab reports. A bar graph is good for comparing things. Below is a bar graph that shows the results of an experiment with paper towels.

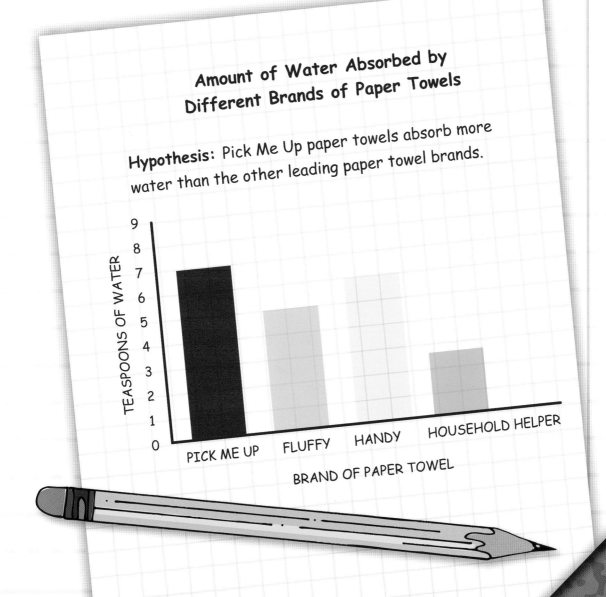

Amount of Water Absorbed by Different Brands of Paper Towels

Hypothesis: Pick Me Up paper towels absorb more water than the other leading paper towel brands.

TEASPOONS OF WATER

9
8
7
6
5
4
3
2
1
0

PICK ME UP   FLUFFY   HANDY   HOUSEHOLD HELPER

BRAND OF PAPER TOWEL

To get a copy of this activity, visit www.cherrylakepublishing.com/activities.

ACTIVITY

Making a Graph

Let's make a sample graph.

HERE'S WHAT YOU'LL NEED:
- Graph paper
- Pencil
- Ruler

INSTRUCTIONS:
1. Write your name at the top of the paper.
2. Create a bar graph using the results of an experiment conducted with magnets and paper clips. The hypothesis stated, "The strength of a magnet determines the number of paper clips it can pick up."
3. Results: Magnet One was the strongest magnet. It picked up 12 paper clips. Magnets Two, Three, and Four were weaker. They picked up 9, 6, and 3 paper clips each.
4. Using the example on page 17 as a guide, write in the title of your graph. Write the number of paper clips along the side of the graph. Write the names of the four magnets at the bottom of the graph.
5. Draw the height of the bar at each magnet to match the number of paper clips that magnet picked up.
6. Color in each of the four bars in your graph.

CHAPTER SIX

Wrapping Things Up

The conclusions section is the final part of your lab report. This is where you compare your hypothesis to the results of your experiment. Was your hypothesis correct? Use your data and observations to explain your findings.

You may also wish to discuss the reasons your results turned out the way they did. It is possible that your methods affected the results. For example, if you ran an experiment that used quantities of liquid, perhaps you used instruments that could not measure them properly. Or if your project was about plant growth, a lack of sunshine or cold temperatures might have affected the results.

ACTIVITY

Add More Information

Add your results and conclusions to the lab report you began in the earlier activities. Include any photographs, charts, and graphs that help explain your data.

To get a copy of this activity, visit www.cherrylakepublishing.com/activities.

What will your next experiment be?

ACTIVITY

Almost Done!

Before you hand in your lab report to your teacher, check everything one more time.

☐ YES ☐ NO Did I write my name and the date on my lab report?

☐ YES ☐ NO Did I write the name of my project title on my lab report?

☐ YES ☐ NO Did I write down my question and hypothesis?

☐ YES ☐ NO Did I describe my experiment carefully?

☐ YES ☐ NO Did I list all the materials and steps I used?

☐ YES ☐ NO Did I record my data accurately?

☐ YES ☐ NO Are the graphs and charts I created easy to understand? Are they properly labeled?

☐ YES ☐ NO Did I clearly state my conclusions?

☐ YES ☐ NO Did I explain if my hypothesis was correct?

☐ YES ☐ NO If my results did not support my hypothesis, did I describe any factors that may have affected the results?

☐ YES ☐ NO Is everything spelled correctly in my lab report?

Did you answer "YES" to all of the questions? Great job!

Glossary

bar graphs (BAHR GRAFS) charts that compare information by showing rectangular bars of different lengths

data (DAY-tuh) information that can be used to plan or make conclusions

hypothesis (hye-PAHTH-uh-sus) an idea that could explain how something works and is tested in an experiment

investigate (in-VES-tuh-gate) to gather information about something

lab report (LAB ri-PORT) a written document that describes and analyzes an experiment that explores a scientific concept

observations (ahb-zur-VAY-shuhnz) things you have noticed by watching carefully

scientific method (sye-uhn-TIF-ik METH-uhd) a way to ask and answer scientific questions by making observations and doing experiments

For More Information

BOOKS

Buczynski, Sandra. *Get Ready for a Winning Science Project.* Ann Arbor, MI: Cherry Lake Publishing, 2012.

Mills, J. Elizabeth. *The Everything Kids' Easy Science Experiments Book: Explore the World of Science Through Quick and Fun Experiments!* Avon, MA: Adams Media, 2010.

WEB SITES

Lab Report Template
www.biologycorner.com/worksheets/labreport.html
Check out some helpful reminders of how to organize your lab reports.

Science Buddies—Steps of the Scientific Method
www.sciencebuddies.org/science-fair-projects/project_scientific_method.shtml
Explore the steps of the scientific method.

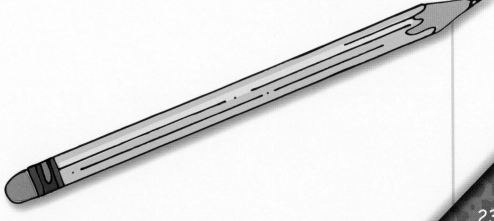

Index

About the Author

Nel Yomtov is an award-winning author of nonfiction books and graphic novels for young readers. He lives in the New York City area.